Dance Mom Survival Guide

Growing a Great Dancer without Losing Your Mind

Malena Lott and Jill Martin

buzz books

Celebrating stories.

Dedicated to our dancer daughters,
Audrey & Hallie.
If it weren't for you, we wouldn't have written
this book in the first place.

table of contents

Introduction by the Authors

Why a dance mom advice book? Why us?

Jill and I decided to write an advice book because we were constantly asking each other – and dance moms who are way more experienced than us – these issues posed in the book. Our first years with company dance daughters were a bit overwhelming. Imagine two dance moms fish-flopping our way through competition season (okay, not **that** fish-flop that our dancers can do! The kind where we're out of our element.) We don't think *you* have to be a fish out of water so we're passing along the advice we've gathered from experts in the field including dance instructors, a dance professor, a psychologist, other dance moms and even dancers themselves.

We've gathered research on dance and also have included some fun lists we think you can relate to, or will relate to someday. The sub-title of the book says it all: *growing a great dancer without losing your mind.* Kids do that to us already. Let's keep what we have left.

We welcome you to the sisterhood of dance moms. We're sitting on our hineys right along with you, and proudly chauffeuring and cheering our dancers on. We swear it's not as dramatic as the reality TV shows, but the emotions are real and the time is intensive. The book is meant to be both humorous and helpful. We hope you'll agree. Bling. It. On.

Jill has a B.A. in Child Development from Harding University. While at Harding, she fell in love with a handsome young man as they served together on a mission trip to Houston's inner city. Soon after, they married and now have four fabulous children, one of whom is a dancer.

Malena Lott is a married mother of three in the Midwest, where she is a dance mom, den mom, brand strategist and author. www.malenalott.com Connect with her @malenalott on Twitter and Instagram and on Facebook at www.facebook.com/malenalottbooks.

Jill and Malena invite you to connect with them on their website at www.dancemomsurvivalguide.com or on Twitter at www.twitter.com/dancesurvival or their Facebook page:

http://www.facebook.com/dancemomsurvivalguide.

chapter 1
First steps in the Dance world

So your child wants to dance; now what?

There's dancing when they are little and they just want to wear tutus and go to class with their friends and they're adorable and we swear we could watch their chubby little legs spin all day in our living room.

And then there's dancing all the time, everywhere, because our daughters have become *possessed by dance* and the tutus now reside in a closet rack next to ballet, jazz, lyrical, modern and tap costumes, right above the mountain of dance shoes. We still love to watch them dance, but if we hear, "Mom, look at my middle leap!" one more time while we're making dinner, we might burst.

This book is about that journey from scenario one to scenario two and beyond. It's a leap, and it's a big one, and it does take lots of time, patience and money. Let's begin at the beginning: why dance?

When they are (were) little, dance may have been our choice for them. After all, parents feel they should pick activities for their children to try and eventually the child will declare whether that activity is right for him/her or not. Dancers may begin in "prince/princess" class or combo classes and if they continue to want to take classes each year and are showing progression in technique and passion, they may have a desire to audition for company or a school dance team. Going from a recreational dancer to a performer is where the shift begins. Dance becomes a part of the dancer's life and therefore a part of the family's life. It happens to all of us.

Top Benefits of Dance

- ✓ Flexibility
- ✓ Strength
- ✓ Balance
- ✓ Endurance (Exercise, good for your heart)
- ✓ Energy
- ✓ Sense of well being (Improves confidence while reducing stress)
- ✓ Artistic pursuit
- ✓ Friendship
- ✓ Boosts Memory

In addition to studies that show the health and social benefits of dance, there are also studies that say children who are involved in team activities make better grades and are less likely to get in to trouble. Makes sense. If your dancer is at the studio or spending weekends at dance competitions, they are busy and making a positive contribution to their well being and to others'.

Dr. Russell, a Ph.D. who founded Choreohealth, lists several benefits of dance. One benefit he suggests is the social aspect. Dance also provides physical activity, which can be enjoyed across a lifetime. In addition, dance (particularly ballet) is very prescriptive and trains dancers in discipline, which in turn provides a foundation for good time management. Dance teaches the principles of diligence and working hard.

More Cool Benefits of Dance

✓ Teaches responsibility.

✓ Teaches teamwork.

✓ Gives children a competitive spirit that comes in handy in the real world.

✓ Never-ending learning. Unlike some sports where the rules are what they are, in dance, participants are constantly learning new moves and choreography and pairing with different dancers so dancing grows with the dancer.

✓ Fosters creativity and entrepreneurship. Watch your dancer's mind expand with possibilities for choreography, finding music that inspires a feeling, which inspires a dance, and raising money for competitions.

✓ Teaches empathy. Many dances also have a story behind them. We've seen stories on bullying, suicide, drunk driving, friendship and more. Dancers are storytellers.

✓   Experience for a career. As you'll see in our last chapter, dance could become a career for them. So far our own dancers (young teens) both aspire to be professional dancers and own their own studios. Whether or not that happens, it's great that what was a hobby has become a bigger dream and gives them a goal.

The Big Picture of Dance in America

Statistics on dance education and careers in dance by National Dance Association, 2010

➢   Schools that Offer Dance as Part of Curriculum: 6,000

➢   Number of private dance studios in the U.S.: 6,000

➢   Students Taught by Qualified part-time and full-time Dance Specialists: 6% (that's 3.5 million out of the 55 million total students)

➢   American Children who Receive Dance Training in School: 43% (36% by physical education teachers, coaches, general educators, volunteers or parents and only 7% by full or part-time specialists)

What should I look for when researching a dance studio?

➢   First, ask yourself what you and your dancer want out of the studio. Is it so your dancer and his/her bestie can hang out dancing for one hour a week? Is it because your dancer now wants to get "serious" about dancing?

➤ Due to your schedule, does it need to be in close proximity to your home? (Remember some classes begin during rush hour so that might impact your decision based on the route.)

➤ Are you new to town? Ask area moms and do some research online. A good studio should at minimum have a website these days, and if it looks like they do a good job communicating and keeping things updated, that's a good sign before you visit.

➤ The studio shouldn't be keeping the staff a secret. The more transparency, the better, including which competitions they go to, awards they have received and the qualifications and photos of their instructors.

➤ How much experience do the instructors have? Do they have dance degrees? Have they – or are they currently – dancing professionally?

➤ Visit the studio and ask for a tour. Typically studios have open houses in the late summer, so try to visit several. Ask questions.

➤ Take our budget sheet with you and don't be afraid to ask the costs upfront. It may appear the class rates are low but costumes or recital fees are very high.

➤ Some studios are recreational only and don't have company/competition classes, so if your dancer wants to compete, that could rule some out.

➤   Ask about age ranges. Some studios focus on young dancers only (say up to 12) so if your child is serious about dance, you might want a studio that includes seniors/advanced dancers.

➤   Ask to see pictures and video of the dance groups so you can see a) what type of costumes the studios pick out and b) styles of choreography. A studio may or may not have that on the website, but it's important to get a glimpse of what "real life" would be for your dancer if they were a part of the studio.

➤   Ask for studio rules and policies. Some studios are stricter than others, including getting there early to warm up and not letting a dancer dance if they don't arrive on time.

What do dance moms and young dancers love about dance?

"I love that it gives my daughter confidence, discipline and stage presence (especially since it's competitive dance - they heavily preach "sassiness"), and it keeps her exercising regularly doing something she loves. I also love that she's getting experience traveling and learning how to positively represent herself and her studio at workshops and competitions. I also love that my daughter is making some fantastic memories and friendships that will last a long time. And of course, I love (most) of the costumes, the makeup and the accessories!"

– Christina Dukeman, dance mom, Edmond, OK, Kim Massay Dance Productions

"That my daughter has the opportunity to learn grace, discipline and structure while still enjoying herself. That she gets to wear dress-up clothes for a purpose. That she can express herself through movement and feel good in her body." – Alice Andress, dance mom, Wichita, KS, MGM

"It helps my son focus on specific goals and then provides ways for him to work hard and achieve those goals. Ultimately, although he goes to competitions, he's not competing against other people-- he's really just competing against himself. When he is working to master a skill, at first his body won't cooperate. He has to spend hours refining his technique, until finally he's able to accomplish what he set his mind to doing. Later, when that skill is performed in front of a judge, if he wins a prize or high score, then he has "won" regardless of how that prize/score compares to the other dancers around him. I also like that he is accountable to other people besides just me and his schoolteachers. His dance teacher will hold him accountable for not getting enough sleep, slacking off, not eating right, not staying organized, being lazy, etc. His studio-mates also hold him responsible. When he's part of a group piece, they all rely on each other to achieve their goals. That's a life lesson that isn't easily learned! – Laura Hogan, dance mom, Allegro West Academy of Dance, Katy, TX

"I love that dance gives my daughter a group of girls to identify with outside of her school environment. When "girl drama" happens at school, dance is a safe alternative." – Cheryl Husmann, dance mom, Edmond, OK, Studio J

"I started my oldest in dance to give her exposure to culture via ballet and classical music, things absent from my own childhood. So, what I loved most about those years at Ballet Oklahoma was the live piano during ballet lessons; her exposure to professional ballerinas and her early exposure to a large stage." – Jennifer James, dance mom, Oklahoma City, OK, McGuinness H.S.

"Getting to learn new dances and performing on stage. I enjoy being on stage because a lot of people see me dance." -Olivia, 10, Dubuque, Iowa, Xtreme Dance

"I love the emotional escape it gives me. It allows me to escape the outside world, leave all my problems behind me and just dance. I love that dance is something that can make people feel. Not just the dancers themselves, but the audience as well are sucked in to the emotions of the dance and the beauty of the music."
– Morgan, 17, Altus, OK, Studio One School of Dance

chapter 2
The Role of a Dance Mom

What does it mean to be a dance mom? The role of "mom" is tough enough, but throw in additional authority figures (instructors, choreographers, studio owners), an expanded peer circle (other dancers on your team and competitors) and additional stress brought on by time, money and competitions, and you've got yourself a whole new (blingy) bag of mama skills.

We asked our diverse DMSG network to help us define it – and master it.

Gretchen Ponio, a dance instructor of eight years in Tulsa, OK and former Miss Dance Oklahoma in 1988 who has been dancing since she was 5, said the number one thing is to, "Encourage your child; don't push or force them to dance if it is not their desire to do so."

She also emphasized the importance of ballet, ballet, ballet. "Ballet technique is the foundation of *all* dance. Too many teachers are having to train or re-train older dancers on how to properly hold or use their bodies. If students would start with good Ballet training before introducing Jazz, Lyrical, or Contemporary/Modern styles of dance, their dance technique and quality would already be there when those styles were introduced. Dancers would be stronger with less injuries. Proper technique and stretching is *key* to all dancers. Ballet is the best way to get that!," says Ponio. She recommends Ballet 2-3 times a week for younger, serious dancers and 3-4 times per week for older ones.

"Find good instructors!" Ponio recommends, "Especially for Ballet. If you have to go to a different school for Ballet training, do it."

Our experience has been most studios recommend at least two Ballet classes a week for company dancers, in addition to 2-3 conventions per year where the dancers get additional training from choreographers who are new to them.

Ponio adds, "Teachers need support from the parent when more training is necessary, specifically referring to Ballet or technique issues."

We second Ponio, and that includes taking additional workshops or classes if a dancer is missing company classes. Please, please don't let your dancer skip class, and if they are not feeling well, but not contagious, they may want to go and sit out and watch so they can keep caught up. If they miss class, they fall behind on choreography and critical practice time that will have to be made up in between so that the dancer doesn't slow the progress of the team. The more in sync, the better.

And last but not least, from Ponio's experience and as a mom to a tween daughter herself, "Dancers need mom's unconditional love and support. (Which is what we all need no matter what we choose to do with our lives, right?)"

We also wanted to hear from someone currently in a dance program at the university level, and we got even more than we asked for. Melissa Motte is a dance major and also a dance instructor for the last two years. Not only do we admire Melissa's attitude, but we're impressed by her work ethic and choreography. Dancers love her.

"As a dancer, some good things a dance mom should know to help their dancer would be to have a clear understanding of the different styles of dance and also really try to understand the difficulty of being a dancer. It is cutthroat out there in the dance world, and the only way to make it is true dedication and commitment from the dancer *and* the mother. Also knowing the styles of dance and knowing what certain dance steps are would help if the dancer asks for your advice," advises Melissa.

"Teachers need moms to understand that we know what we are doing. (smiles) Remember, we are the dance instructors, we are where your daughters are trying to get to, and we have been where they are now. But some dance moms feel they know more than we do. I'm different from most teachers. If a dance mom tries to argue they know more, I suggest they come try and teach my class (smiles)."

"What a dancer needs from their mom is just for them to be there. Understanding how stressful it is, understanding how competitions work, being there to record certain steps, and of course, to be supportive."

Dance Mom and former champion Union Varsity Highstepper Kari Ernest weighs in on the role of a dance mom. "As a former dancer, and now a dance mom, my best advice for moms is to be realistic and understand your boundaries. We all believe our daughters are beautiful and talented, but as we praise their strengths, we must also acknowledge their weaknesses. No dancer is perfect, there is always room for improvement, and no matter how talented the dancer, there will always be someone better. Learning to accept criticism and deal with disappointment is so important in the development of a dancer, and it is the job of teachers/coaches to turn our daughters into the best dancers they can be."

"It's so easy to let the 'Mama Bear' come out when our daughters are disappointed, feeling picked on, or don't get a part they think they deserve. But, for the most part, teachers/coaches are doing what they think is best for the dancers and the team. Our job as moms is to soften the blow a bit, help our daughters to overcome the let-downs, encourage them to work harder, and use the experience to not only make them stronger dancers, but stronger people as well."

Child and family psychologist Dr. Lisa Marotta discussed the importance of parents being healthy role models when it comes to dance and teaching important life skills that the child will carry with them throughout adulthood.

"It's the mom's role to provide guidance," said Dr. Marotta. "Sometimes you lead and sometimes you follow. In any competitive sport, nothing happens without a supporting person. Kids don't have the maturity to be goal-focused, so parents can provide the encouragement and look at the bigger picture."

Dr. Marotta says our role is helping our dancers evaluate and revaluate what they are expecting to get from dance. "Sometimes we get sidetracked because boundaries get blurred. Perhaps we're leading too far ahead or we lack the objectivity that we need to have."

Getting too caught up in the drama could include, "trashing the mentor or taking down the other competition, which isn't good role-modeling," says Dr. Marotta. Being a good role model also means the mom being able to handle stress well and having good life skills of her own. She warns moms not to undermine the authority of the teacher or disrupt the camaraderie and unity in the dancers.

Which is the main emphasis on reality shows, isn't it? Pitting moms against the teacher, moms trash-talking other moms, and dancers against each other, provides the conflict necessary for a reality show, but it's not the way things should work in the real world.

When asked about the "reality" television program *Dance Moms*, Dr. Russell mentioned that it is important to ensure that the attitudes toward emotional and physical health portrayed on the show are rejected by those who are serious about developing young dancers. "Even allowing for the fact that the program is supposed to be entertainment rather than a true depiction of dance training, parents must not blindly relegate authority for their children's teaching to those who do not respect the children or the parents, or who teach unsafe technique and exercises. I do not advocate hovering or meddling parents (because typically they become very annoying and counterproductive when they interfere with the well-intended, proper instruction of their children). But, it is important for parents to be aware of the environment where their children are taught and for teachers and parents to work together for the wholesome benefit of the children."

Dance Instructor Melissa Motte sees some reality in reality TV. "Some teachers believe that all of *Dance Moms* is fake, or they are so mean. I disagree. Some of it is for TV of course. Sometimes people forget that, but not all of it is fake. Abby (the owner and star of the show) may be mean sometimes, and I disagree with some of her ways, but strict teachers make great disciplined dancers! In the real world, which I'm currently trying to make it in as a dancer, they don't pat you on your back! They are blunt, and if you don't make the cut, you're out! At some studios I've been to it was black leotard and pink tights to ballet, sports bra and spanks to jazz. If the teachers couldn't see your lines, you were told to change clothes or go home. If you didn't have the correct outfit for ballet, you were sent home. If you even talked in Ballet or rehearsal, there wasn't a 'Everyone listen up!', you were sent home! It is like that in college classes now. If I walk in right when ballet class starts, I'm not allowed in the classroom. You are to be stretching 5 minutes before class starts. In professional companies, they are stretching *30 minutes before class*! You have to be DISCIPLINED. Abby does go overboard sometimes, but she is preparing them for the real world in some ways. And as you see, she makes GREAT dancers! Now, you do not have to yell at your kids and say hurtful comments, but again, people have to remember just because it says REALITY show, all of it isn't REAL! But you have to have rules. If they are broken, there are consequences. Abby does that!"

As dance moms, one of our favorite things about writing this book is hearing from all points of view to help us help our dancers.

Dr. Russell's most important piece of advice for dance moms:

"<u>Do not,</u> under any circumstances, turn your son or your daughter blindly over to dance teachers, presuming they are experts and are going to know what is best for your son or daughter. There is nothing more important than that. You've got to know how qualified the teachers are. You've got to know who your kids are with because the kids aren't their responsibility, they are *your* responsibility as their parent."

He adds, "Trophies in the trophy case don't always tell the whole story. Make sure you know what is going on with your kids…get in there and find out."

Dance Mom Alice urges moms to control their tongues. "Moms, please don't be competitive or compare children (at least not out loud). Dance is a fun outlet for kids. They're all learning something new, about dance and their bodies. At some point it can and will become competitive, but don't start out that way," says Alice.

Seven-year Dance Mom veteran, Rhonda Garrison, from Altus, OK offers this advice for moms. "Don't try to fulfill your dreams through your daughter or son. If they are in dance, it is because they love it -- dance is too much hard work for those who do not love it. Be supportive, be encouraging, be available to listen (be on time to pick them up after practice), but let the dance teacher do his or her job."

Lauren echoed that sentiment in her caution of using "we." "When I write or talk about his dance (on Facebook, talking to friends, etc.) I strive to keep my pronouns in check. It's not 'WE went to an audition', it's 'He went'. It's not 'Our dance teacher said...', it's 'HIS dance teacher said...'. The pronouns may seem trivial, but it helps me remember that his dancing belongs to HIM."

Are you a crafty mom? Rhonda thinks it's a good idea to "Learn to sew, always keep supplies on hand, and develop a talent for thinking on your feet -- once in a while that skill will save a routine. Though it's hard sometimes with so many personalities, try to stay out of drama. There may be someone (or several someones) annoying to you; still, try to avoid conflict. The dressing room is no place for temper tantrums or hurt feelings. Most of all, *learn to go with the flow*. I learned very quickly that creative people are not always the most organized, and sometimes they make last-minute changes when inspiration hits. It's okay. These things happen. Just go with it," says Rhonda.

Whew. Thanks, Rhonda. *Go with the flow*. We're on it!

Dance Mom Lauren adds, "Help your child learn to be his/her own advocate. If he/she has a problem with a teacher, coach your child in how to approach the teacher to discuss it. If you always go to the teacher for your child, then the teacher will start to see you as a "problem parent", and you've really done your child a disservice in not teaching him/her to tackle the problem himself/herself!"

Dance Mom Kari wishes someone would've told her just how much parental involvement is necessary nowadays. "My daughter is on the same dance team as I was in high school, and my parents weren't nearly as involved. They were supportive and did whatever they needed to do, but the coach didn't rely on parents as much back then. Now it seems that parents run almost the entire program, and it can be extremely time-consuming. Dance team has taken over my family's life, and while we enjoy it and wouldn't change a thing, it was a bit of a surprise," says Kari.

It's that kind of fair warning we aim to give parents with this book.

Dance Mom Jennifer regrets that she let her daughter quit dance for awhile and encourages giving your dancer extra support. "If your daughter becomes self-conscious during adolescence, spend the money on private lessons. Don't let her quit unless she just hates it. Find a studio that doesn't force your girl to wear skimpy clothes, etc. Consult privately with the studio about your unique challenges. I didn't press hard enough, and my daughter quit for two years. She was an amazing dancer. I'm glad she's picking it back up."

The most difficult part of dance for Dance Mom Lauren? "Waiting, and waiting, and waiting. We wait outside the studio. We wait in the audience until they are on stage. We wait until the results come in. We wait (often impatiently!) until they finally learn that elusive skill, but the moment they do there is suddenly some new skill we are waiting for them to learn."

Dancer Olivia Jones, 10, who has been dancing since she was 3, had this advice for dance moms: "Moms, don't get stressed out with your kids because that just gets the kids worried and more stressed than they already may be."

Great advice, Olivia.

chapter 3
Dressing a Dancer

Booty shorts and bling. Tights and tutus. Bobby pins, bobby pins and more bobby pins. Dance is beautiful in its own right, but a performance comes alive with costumes that help tell the story. And dance classes alone require perfunctory apparel that helps the dancer move. We'll also touch on the moral debate on costumes – how little is too much? *Are we dressing little girls too provocatively?*

One of the first things we learned as new dance moms is that different styles of dance require different clothing and that quality and fit matter.

Carolyn Windsor, Owner of Show Biz Dancewear Boutique, in Oklahoma City, took us through her recommendations and insight for dancewear.

"Most of what a dancer needs to wear is determined by the studio they attend. They often have specific brands, colors, and styles they want their dancers to wear. The top brands in basic tap, ballet, and jazz shoes are Bloch and Capezio," says Windsor.

She cautions against discount stores. "One big mistake moms make is trying to find dance shoes at discount stores. They are just not as good quality and usually the knock-off shoes cost the same as the better quality brands," Windsor explains.

Windsor's Dance Shoes 101

✓   Dance shoes are made to be a covering for the foot and fit as close as possible so it shows off the foot. Obviously, little girls who are still growing will need a little growing room, but as they get older you want shoes to fit tightly.

✓   Pointe – Find the brand and style that fits the dancer's foot best. There are many styles of Pointe shoes within each brand. When you fit for Pointe, you are fitting the shape of the toes, length, and the strength of the shank. Dancers with more of an arch in their foot need a stronger shank. Allow plenty of time for fitting Pointe shoes because you may have to try several shoes on before you find the one for your foot.

✓   Tap – Most tap shoes fit like a standard shoe. Younger, less experienced tappers can start with the riveted or nailed tap shoes (up to about 7-or-8-years-old). The best sound, however, comes from tap shoes with screws. Some like the single screw Capezio. Traditional tappers often prefer the 3-screw tap shoes. Intermediate tappers should move to the screwed tap shoes. Cloggers have completely different shoes that jingle.

✓ Jazz – One of the best sellers is Bloch slip-on jazz shoe. It comes in two styles: elastic V and microfiber around the arch. Which style you prefer will depend on the shape of the dancer's foot.

✓ Lyrical – In Lyrical and Contemporary dance, dancers may either go barefoot or wear Footundeez or a similar brand, which enable them to spin and leap without the risk of slipping.

Tights and **leotards** are dancewear standards because they are fitting to the body and have stretch that allows the dancer to move. Another a-ha for us was the different types of tights available (and we don't just mean color). Windsor recommends, "Usually you just go with what your studio tells you to get. Top selling tights are Bloch, Capezio, and Danskin."

Windsor's Tips on Leotards

✓ Each leotard differs in size by brand/style.

✓ Torso length determines the size you need. You need to try on a leotard before you buy because there is such a difference in each leotard.

✓ Don't be concerned about the size you have to get. Most people can fit into any size leotard, it just depends on how high you want the legs cut. You need to make sure the bottom doesn't sag!

✓ Bottom line (pun intended): "Forget about size – go with what looks and feels best."

Some instructors may allow the dancers to wear t-shirts and sweatpants to class, as well as booty shorts without tights underneath. In hip hop, dancers can typically wear whatever they can move in and it purposely has a more "street" feel to it. Hip hop shoes are often high-tops.

Underwear. We're kidding. You don't wear underwear under leotards during competition. The instructors will not let them go on stage with underwear underneath their costume for practical reasons. Not only can you see lines, but often we can see the peek-a-boo of the underwear, which is distracting and unnecessary since leotards and tights are meant to be worn without. However, many dancers still wear underwear during leotards during class, so just ask the instructor what the rules are regarding undergarments.

Bras. Dancers need special bras to be worn under leotards and costumes. You may be able to find sports bras with the correct straps, but often you'll need bras for performance, too, which may include clear straps. We feel for the big-chested dancers because support is important so our eyes are on the dance and not on the chest. Definitely worth the investment to get something that works for your dancer while she's in motion.

Toiletries. We recommend packing your dancer's bag with the appropriate toiletries for class as well as competitions. Deodorant, body spray, body wipes – all important so your child doesn't feel self-conscious about all that sweating and body odor.

Periods. We haven't been to a competition yet where one of our dancers didn't start her period unexpectedly. Since most dancers have smart phones, ask them to download an app such as Monthly Cycles or iPeriod Free so they'll have a better idea of when Aunt Flo will be visiting. If your daughter has irregular periods, that won't be foolproof, but keeping track helps. Nonetheless, always pack tampons in case you get a surprise (this would go for tweens who haven't started their first period, either).

Also, your daughter may want to learn how to use tampons before performance season and consider using the "super" to ensure no leaks happen if it's tough to get to the bathroom each hour if it's a heavy flow day.

Ah, costumes, the stuff of shine, bling and tulle.

Dancers require a costume for each performance, and expect that it will be new. Fit is extremely important for costumes because with all the moving and positions they do on stage, wardrobe malfunctions are a big issue. Clasps have a funny way of unclasping. (And last year, two of our dancers' clasps came undone during the exact same move and it was tough for the lyrical costume to stay on and not roll off the shoulder during the rest of the performance. Solution: Always safety pin around clasps or snaps.)

Instructors and studio owners select the costumes way ahead of time. Dancers have to be measured and fitted, and the costumes may have to be altered. Nothing adds to stress like not getting costumes in on time. Ill-fitting costumes draw the eye away from the performance, so it's important to make adjustments to ensure it fits all the dancers the way it should.

Do moms get input on costumes? No. The studios have to make sure no two instructors pick the same costume for dances (and yes, there have been battles), and for recital that could mean forty or fifty costumes plus however many costumes are necessary for competitions. That's a lot of tulle. See below for advice on revealing costumes.

How much do costumes cost? It depends, but can vary from $100 to $200 on average. Most studios will ask for half-up front and then the second half during the second semester for recital costumes. Company costumes are typically billed during the month it was ordered or received, depending on how the studio manages it. Hip hop costumes might cost less because you can get elements at discount stores, such as T-shirts and sweatpants, but accessories can add up.

Elements of a costume could include:

✓   Special tights

✓   Hair pieces (and bobby pins!)

✓   Wrist or arm pieces

✓   Special earrings

✓   Special shoes (though often if you have beige or black jazz shoes you may be covered. Hip hop will normally all buy one type of street shoe so they match).

You can see how it adds up. Remember to put it on your budget sheet.

Other Gear (You Just Thought You Were Done)

✓   Dance bag (The more classes they take, the more specific bag you may need.)

✓   Cosmetics kit if in Company or Dance Team (Caboodle)

✓   Water bottles

✓   Healthy snacks

✓   Cosmetics (The instructor will have brands and colors they prefer so the dancers match on stage.)

Dance Instructor Melissa emphasizes the importance of having a back-up plan. "I was always taught to have a Plan A: The costume you ordered and a Plan B: One your mom made for back-up. Ha. That helps a lot. If something spills on a costume, you'll have a back up! Also, hair pieces: pinned in the head! I cannot stress that enough! Also practice in the costumes once or twice just to make sure there aren't any problems," advises Melissa.

She also recommends a foam roller for muscles and tennis balls for cramps in backs or legs. "Icy Hot. Also, a Theraband to stretch out hips and feet!"

On Revealing/Provocative Costumes

Two things incite the biggest reactions and debate for dance moms.

The first is provocative dancing. The next is provocative/revealing costumes. We touched on the first in the chapters on finding a studio and in our competitions chapter. When it comes to costumes, interestingly, the dance itself may not be sexually provocative in terms of the lyrics or dance moves (come hither or even lustful expressions), yet the costume can be. But some of that may be in the eye of the beholder and based on how conservative one's views are when it comes to costumes.

For example, some moms don't want their dancers in two-pieces whatsoever, so it would be important for them to know what type of costumes the studio puts the girls in. In some cases the studio may have a leotard on some girls and a bra or halter version for those who either look good in it or feel comfortable in it. Body type plays a big role in that. A dancer who is either big-chested or heavier on top wouldn't want to dance around in a bra and booty shorts anymore than the instructor would want them to.

Or would they? If you look at what kids and teens wear in everyday life, it's surprising what they'll wear, even when it doesn't fit them or flatter them. So our dancers are not the best judge on that. If you are uncomfortable with what your dancer will be wearing, speak to the instructor upfront so that something can be done about it (before there is no time to order something different.)

A costume might have complete coverage and still be provocative. At every competition, you will likely see things on stage that you feel are better left for the bedroom or adulthood, but to some extent, it comes with the territory.

A dance instructor who prefers to remain anonymous, has this to say about it:

"I'm a rather conservative teacher and mother of a tween who loves to dance and cheer. The world of competitive dance lends itself to a rather provocative style of dance and costuming. I will not allow my daughter to compete with our studio because of the costume choices and style of dance they are being taught. Today's dance competitions have young dancers clad in not much more than bra tops and tiny skirts. I'm not an advocate for skimpy clothing, so I don't approve of the costuming in general these days. Many dances that I have watched at competitions look like they are more appropriate for a strip club than a dance competition. It's really sad to me that this has become a norm. For those reasons, I have opted to stay out of the competition part of our studio. I'm trying to teach my daughter to honor God with her body, not objectify herself. I wish our studio would hold itself to higher standards, but they just seem to follow the trends. Like I said, this is a norm."

At a recent competition, we talked with another anonymous dance mom on her view of costumes and we discussed the *Dance Mom* episode where the girls (as young as 8 years old) wore nude-colored leotards, so from the audience they appeared naked on stage. The perception the viewer gets on the show is that Abby Miller, the star of the show and studio owner/choreographer, does those things to get attention. And reality shows, in particular, love for their "star" to do anything that will create more buzz, which in turn creates more viewers, happy advertisers, and so on.

If you have a problem with your dancer of any age shaking her booty, shimmying her shoulders or gyrating her hips, you may not be comfortable with dance no matter where your child dances. You will not be the choreographer or get approval of any routine, which is why picking the studio you feel is the best fit for you is important, but beyond that, it's out of your control. Sure, you can pull your dancer from a routine (or studio) but to some extent you may always be out of your comfort zone.

Jazz and musical theater can be very sassy, lyrical and contemporary can be extremely romantic or sensual and hip-hop is booty-full. Dancing requires us to separate our child from the dancer. Just like an actress, the "person" should disappear, replaced by the character he/she is playing. That's hard for parents because we see our child. Dance is supposed to be an art.

Our role as dance moms may be to monitor and make sure our dancers are safe, but that doesn't mean there won't be cringe-worthy choreography, bad performances and drama that's out of our control. In addition to some dancing we may find provocative, there is also awkward choreography, outlandish props and just plain boring dancers. At a certain point (it won't take long) – you'll have seen it all.

Dance as an art can be in the eye of the beholder. One person may love performances to worship songs where props are Bibles. Another might find that preachy or even silly. Sometimes something works on one level and fails on another. And before we judge too harshly, have we tried to choreograph? It's not easy. (And as Dance Instructor Melissa said earlier, just go try to choreograph her class!)

At the end of the day, the dancers are there to show off their skills and prove to the judges they get it. You are not going to like everything you see that your dancer is in or what you see other studios do.

As Dance Mom Cheryl says, "The studios that promote more 'provocative' dances aren't your problem. Just get used to the shock and focus on your dancer."

You may only like a small percentage of what you see, but the good news is, *you do not have to watch the other performances if you don't want to*. Make the decision that's right for your family, but that might mean having to stretch your comfort zone, too.

But if you don't watch, what will you talk about with the other moms in the lobby?

And speaking of moms, what should we wear to these things? Is there a rule? A dress code? We thought we'd have some fun with this one.

Dance Mom Attire

✓ **Twinkie Dance Moms** dress like their dancers. Sure, some may also be the choreographer or studio owner, but we see lots of dance moms who "twinkie" dress like the girls, including sparkly ribbons and matching tracksuit.

✓ **Shirt Says So Dance Moms**. If walking around with a girl in a dance costume isn't obvious enough, your shirt, hat or jacket telling us you are a dance mom should make it clear.

✓ **Studio Junkie Moms.** It's nice to be supportive of the studio you are representing – team spirit! – and if you don't want the same shirts the dancers are wearing, there may be a more conservative option for you that lets you show studio pride without looking like you're going to leap down the lobby.

✓ **Boob Bling Moms.** We couldn't resist pointing out the number of sparkly busts we see roaming the convention centers. We know the dancers like to add sparkle to everything, but we were surprised by the amount of bling on the headlights. We see your girls, and you know which girls we're talking about. (Related: Booty Bling and Cap Bling)

✓ **Stiletto Moms.** These moms aren't about to let five-inch heels slow them down. They put fashion above practicality and bring their shoe collection with them at competitions.

✓ **Come-As-You-Are Moms.** And there are mamas who look like they just rolled out of bed and barely made it on time. Some moms wait and "get ready" at the convention hall or along with their dancers in the dressing room. It's okay. We've all been there.

Most importantly, we want you to be happy and comfortable. If that means wearing boob bling or stilettos or comfy sweatpants, more power to you.

chapter 4
The Healthy Dancer

How fit does my child need to be to dance?

How fit will it make her/him?

Most common dance injuries and how to prevent them.

What if my child gets hurt? Can they still dance?

What about diet and exercise outside of dance class?

How old does my child need to be to dance on Pointe?

Health and fitness is a primary concern when it involves an activity as physically intense as dance.

Dr. Jeff Russell, dance medicine and science professor and researcher at Ohio University, who has more credentials than we can shake a baton at (B.A. Sports Medicine, Rice University; M.S. Sports Medicine, University of Arizona; Ph.D. Dance Medicine & Science, University of Wolverhampton, UK, and a member of the Board of Directors of the International Association for Dance Medicine & Science) created Choreohealth, a curriculum which provides dance health information to studio owners, dancers, schools with dance programs, and parents. The Choreohealth seminar provides to young dancers and their parents much of the same information he taught in a college course at the University of California, Irvine. All kinds of information on dance health can be found on his website www.choreohealth.com. Another great source for dance health information is the International Association for Dance Medicine & Science website www.iadms.org.

Dr. Russell provided us with some in-depth information that can help dance moms understand the scope of health concerns and injuries for dancers. Not to scare us, of course, but to prepare us and to help them on their journey.

Before we get to the injuries related to dancing, we think it's important to stress how healthy dancing can be. Dancing provides amazing cardiovascular workouts as well as endurance, strength and flexibility. Our favorite online resource for calories burned by dancing is fitnessblender.com.

Calories burned varies by your dancer's size, but according to the site, for dancers 120-190 pounds, hip hop burns 370-690 calories per hour.

Ballet can burn from 380-450 calories per hour, and it also works to improve the core, which is important for posture and strength. (Which is why football players have been known to do ballet strength exercises!)

Depending on pace, livestrong.com tells us tap dancing can burn approximately 316 calories per hour.

An Interview with Dr. Jeff Russell

According to Dr. Jeff Russell of Ohio University, many in the medical profession do not know how to deal with dancers, a research topic he presented at the 2012 International Association for Dance Medicine & Science Annual Meeting in Singapore.

Typically, doctors say, "Just stop dancing if it hurts." Many doctors lack an understanding of the physical requirements of dance, so dancers get frustrated and storm out of the doctor's office and go back to dancing and deal with the pain. Sometimes stopping is appropriate (such as with a stress fracture), and a support system is key at this point.

What injuries are dancers most susceptible to?

Dancers are most susceptible to lower extremity injuries. The most common injuries are ankle sprains, and overuse injuries (especially in the feet) such as tendon pains (flexor hallucis longus and Achilles') and stress fractures in the feet. Dancers can also experience knee pain under the kneecap and snapping hips. Sometimes discomfort is not a big deal, but when there is pain it can be a big deal and needs to be looked after.

What symptoms should parents be looking for?

✓ Pain – a signal in the body that tells the dancer there is something going on that needs attention. "Dancing through pain" never works.

✓ The difference between discomfort and pain is critical. When discomfort turns into pain then something needs to be done. A qualified professional needs to look at the injury. This is difficult because dancers (high-school and upward) often wear a badge of courage and endure the pain.

✓ Parents should teach young dancers to know it is okay to alert others when they are in pain. When problems arise things can actually be done to help with the pain and enable the dancer to improve.

Ways to Avoid Injury

"What we tell the dancers is you need to be engaging in physical training in addition to your technical training. There is always such an emphasis on technical training. What is dance? It is a beautiful art form, and you get better at it by doing it again and again and again. Unfortunately, that much repetition causes the body to break down, and the body is not able to withstand the demands that you are putting on it."

"If you would spend a little bit of the time you are spending on technical training and instead spend it on physical training, on strengthening, on musculoskeletal endurance, on cardiovascular endurance, then actually the body works better, and the technical aspects of the dance become a whole lot better."

"Your body as a tuned machine, if you will, is able to perform at a higher level and do the things that you want it to do aesthetically because you are in better physical condition in addition to technical condition. It is definitely important for dancers to engage in cross training."

We're piping in here to add that this is why good dance studios spend a good portion of the class on warm-ups, stretches and exercises. If your dancer is getting good workouts outside of dance class they'll have the physical endurance and stretching required in dance. The 20-minutes of cardio rule for every day they aren't in class is a baseline that could help you set up a physical fitness regiment for them outside of class. They'll be that much more ahead. Some young dance stars spend as much as two hours a day stretching before they begin their routines. Wow!

Is there an age that is too early to start dancing?

"Early on, dancing needs to be fun. Little kids need to just have fun with it and enjoy it so that they are not burned out on it when they get older. But as they progress, what you need are people who are wise about what they are doing with their dancers. When you put a dancer on Pointe and she's not strong enough and her skeleton cannot support her, you're asking for a lot of trouble. You can't just say, 'It's an age thing.' If you start them too early there can be a problem because the strength that is most important is not there. In addition, bones are trying to grow and growth plates are trying to close; if you don't have the strength to support the feet and the ankles and the legs, you are going to end up with a real problem. There are a number of cases where dancers have had to quit Pointe altogether because they started too early and were injured."

Note: Dr. Russell does a pre-Pointe evaluation, which evaluates strength, range of motion, and amount of time spent dancing. He won't even consider someone before they are at least 11-years-old, but once a dancer reaches age 11, she must be evaluated on a variety of factors that are related to successful Pointe work.

Time in class. Limit time per day?

"There is no easy answer. There are a lot of factors to consider, but, as a rule of thumb, if a dancer is going more than 3 hours a day, he/she may need to think about backing off a bit. There are more important things than dance, namely family and school." Dr. Russell takes a "whole-person" view of wellness and life activities, but it's an individual question for families. "Physically, more than three hours a day can wear a person out and you have to have rest, sleep, eat well and drink lots of water."

Diet and Nutrition

Good quality nutrition is important for all of us, but it's especially important to make sure our dancers are eating healthily. Instead of simple carbs, dancers need complex carbs. Dr. Russell recommends restricting white potatoes, pasta, rice, and especially sugar. Simple carbs aren't good for fuel or weight control, and they turn on molecular and genetic keys that addict people to simple carbs. Several smaller, high quality meals throughout the day are better than the typical three (or sometimes fewer) daily meals. In the mid-morning and mid-afternoon, nuts and raisins or other dried fruit (not trail mix with M&M's) is a good choice. Dancers also need plenty of protein. (Also visit DanceMomSurvivalGuide.com for our Dance Forever Mix. You'll want to eat it, too!)

- ✓ Water – 500 ml (down a half dozen of these a day)
- ✓ Fruits and veggies
- ✓ A good breakfast (whole grain), mid-morning snack, lunch, afternoon snack (nuts, dried fruit, but not a lot of dried fruit b/c of sugar)
- ✓ PBJ is not too bad because of the peanut butter's protein, but the sugar content is high. Use whole-grain bread and natural peanut butter without added sugar.
- ✓ Read labels because so many foods are loaded with sugar and other undesirable ingredients. Note that foods labeled "healthy" do not necessarily contain healthy ingredients. It is critical for dancers and dance parents to be good nutrition consumers.
- ✓ Parents need to take a leadership role.

Dr. Russell suggests a sample script for parents regarding their child's healthy eating: "We're eating this. When you get hungry enough, I'm sure you'll learn to like it. This is good for you, and it will fuel your body for the activity that you love to do."

"If nutrition is right, so many other things go right -- weight, brain function, relationships, and school work. So much hinges on nutrition."

Foods or drinks may appear to be healthy, but have hidden sugars. Check out Dr. Mark Hyman's website at drhyman.com. He's a functional-medicine physician in Boston who helps people through nutrition and has even changed the diabetic state of patients through healthy eating. Dr. Hyman also has an emergency food pack that may give beneficial ideas for dancers and dance parents who are committed to good health.

Advice from a Dance Professor

Dance professor Kathleen Redwine who teaches at the University of Oklahoma gave this advice. "Dancers need to take care of themselves, on many levels. Physically, the basics are very important: stay hydrated, eat healthy foods in healthy amounts and get enough rest. Other exercise is also important, like walking, yoga, pilates, and so on. Staying positive and happy helps a lot, and that's where moms and dads can offer so much support."

Dance instructor Gretchen adds that her favorite health/fitness product for dancers for resistance training is Therabands also known as Resistabands. "They are stretchy bands of rubber of various densities that are a great tool for resistance training. I love to use them in my classes!" says Gretchen.

That's two votes for Therabands if you're counting.

Since our experts all highly recommended daily exercise outside of studio time, we recommend helping your dancer set up a fitness routine outside of class. That could include enrolling them in a Pilates or Yoga class or doing that at home (even with you!) or other fitness activities such as walking or biking. Ask your dance instructor about any activities your dancers should avoid. Some studios, especially ballet, do not want the dancers to run due to the change in muscle tone as well as the hardship on the joints, especially the knees.

Advice for Ankle/Foot Injuries

As Dr. Russell said, ankle and foot injuries are the most common injuries for dancers.

As with all injuries, it's important to get it looked at by a professional to see if anything was fractured or broken and the right course of treatment is followed to encourage speedier recovery and prevent a worse injury. The following is NOT medical advice, just general information about treatment options.

According to several medical resources, the most common method for treatment for ankle injuries from twisting to spraining is RICE.

Rest The first 24-48 hours are critical so putting as little weight on the injured ankle as possible is important.

Ice Using an ice pack for twenty minutes every few hours for the first 48 hours is the general advice.

Compression Using an ankle wrap or brace is recommended to keep the ankle stable. These are available at local drugstores. Keep it snug, but not so tight it cuts off circulation.

Elevate Keep the foot elevated above the heart (such as on a pillow on the couch or in the bed).

If symptoms don't improve steadily over the next week or so, you may have a tear or fracture that may need an X-ray or boot or crutches.

Chapter 5
First Leap - From Dancer to Team or Company Dancer

Dancers may take multiple classes a week at a studio and only perform in the end-of-year showcase or recital, which will be on stage in front of weepy parents and proud grandparents. However, if a recreational dancer wants to be more involved in dance, they may audition for Company, which is the group that travels and competes in regional and then a national competition.

The other option is the dancer may try out for a competitive dance team at their middle school or high school. The latter example could be jazz dancers, Highsteppers or pom pom dancers. Some schools may choose not to compete and only be a performance squad that entertains the crowds at games or at half-time performances and may perform in the community.

While team try-outs are typically held in late spring before school is out, Company auditions are generally held at the end of the summer before the fall session begins. Your dancer would learn a routine and audition with other dancers so that the instructors could see how dancers mesh and so they could ascertain skill level.

Company auditions may feel daunting the first time, but it's the only way studios can determine where the dancer is in his/her journey. Dancers progress at their pace, which can be quickly or much more slowly. That's how you see 8-year-olds on YouTube who are more skilled than many 18-year-old dancers. Age is not as much of a predictor of skill as experience and time devoted to dance.

Two biggies when it comes to Company:
- ✓ Financial Investment – Brace Yourself
- ✓ Time Investment – Warm Your Tush

More specific? Here's our readiness list.

Checklist for Team or Company Readiness:

✓ Your dancer loves it and wants to dance all the time and continues to improve.

✓ Your dancer and your family is committed to the time requirements of Company or a Dance Team, which can include many afternoon and evenings of dance and many weekends devoted to conventions and competitions, especially in the spring and summer. This could mean dropping other activities because there could be time conflicts.

✓ Your dancer understands he/she would need to dance year around, including the summer to stay flexible, work on technique, and continue to improve.

✓   Your family is willing to make the financial commitment necessary to compete. (See our Dance Budget

✓   Sheet below.)

✓   At least one parent or responsible party has the time to drive the dancer to and from class or practice, and depending on their age, sit and wait on them.

✓   On the emotional readiness level, your dancer would need to be able to take critiques for improvement and work on technique to keep up with the rest of the team.

How old does my dancer need to be to try out for Company?

Though different studios have varying names for it, Company can start as young as 5-years-old, with petite or mini-company dancers, and typically goes up to senior dancers. After that, dancers may decide to major in dance in college or move on to perform with a professional dance company. Many competitions include an adult category, too.

How are Company groups determined?

The studio will match skill sets and whom they believe will dance best together. If you live in a big city and have a big studio, you could have multiple company groups all within the same age range. For competitions, studios enter the dancers in categories based on the level of dance and how many hours they take in classes each week. Some competitions may have beginner, intermediate and advanced dancer categories and others may only have two, or even combine them if they have low entries.

Dance Mom Lauren, whose son has been dancing seriously for four years, had a lot of great advice about studios and helping steer your child into the right place.

"Once your child is about 10 or 11, you need to help your child decide on his/her focus. If that focus is lyrical/contemporary/hip hop, then a competition studio with lots of trophies is a great place to be! However, if the focus is on ballet, then it's time to leave that competition studio and get to a classical ballet training center. By this age, kids who want to become ballet dancers need at least four 1.5 hour ballet technique classes a week plus twice a week pre-Pointe or Pointe. These classes should be used for only technique-- not rehearsals or learning tricks. Competition studios very rarely offer this type of ballet training. If you wait until 12 or 13 to make the switch from competition dance to ballet, then your child will be very behind! Here is a link to ballet training expectations: http://dancers.invisionzone.com/index.php?showtopic=54927

"How can you tell if you're getting good ballet training? First, look at the hour expectations in the above link. Second, ask about a syllabus. If there isn't a set syllabus (e.g., RAD, Cecchetti, Vaganova, ABT), then ask about the method/syllabus that most influences the teacher. Third, look at the Summer Intensives (SIs) the teenage students attend and how frequently they receive scholarships to the SIs. A studio with excellent ballet training should have students receiving scholarship to SI's associated with large ballet companies. Fourth, look at the competitions. Ballet studios generally don't participate in a lot of dance competitions other than ballet-only competitions such as YAGP. If they do compete in mainstream dance competitions, it's usually just their 8-12 year olds, as the older students are putting their focus on preparing for SI (Summer Intensive) auditions."

on the male dancer

In her interview, Lauren brought up another important point that moms of male dancers can relate to and moms of female dancers witness everywhere we go: *male dancer worship*. I mean, there are so few of them! And look how darling they are! How strong, how flexible! We'd love for our daughters to get to dance with more guys in routines, and what about the "boy bonus points" you hear about at competitions? Nothing makes your dance stand out like having a male in the mix.

But…but. A heed of warning from Lauren who has seen that worship aplenty, for good and ill.

"Don't treat male dancers as commodities. Don't treat them as royalty. You do them no favors by treating them any differently than the girls. We went to five studios before we settled into one that we loved. The other studios oohed and ahhhed over my son, and treated him like he was made of gold. Being treated like a prince may be fun for awhile, but it quickly gets old and it's very hard to respect a studio that continues with that type of treatment. Ultimately, the studio that we stayed at for the past four years is the one that made no big deal of his maleness and just treated him like everyone else," says Lauren.

Got it. We will try to keep our "oohs and aahs" in check. Thanks for bringing this to our attention, Lauren. We appreciate your candor.

Dance mom Christina Dukeman, whose tween daughter has been competing for three years, suggests, "Find another mom or two you feel comfortable with - someone you can travel with, whom you can trust to watch your daughter when you can't (or just need a break), and someone to laugh at it all with you. Also, always have tissues, bobby pins, safety pins, and extra hairspray! Keep your sense of humor - you and your daughter will need it, and let's face it: sometimes it's just funny when someone's hair feather falls off during a performance, or when you look up in the dressing room and can't see through the fog of hairspray and glitter, or when hotel security dumps a drunk, passed-out stranger in your room and you discover him after a long day of competition. (Yes, that really happened to us)."

In fact, we agree so much with the Dance Mom BFF mindset, that we've included an extra chapter at the end of the book with ideas on how dance moms can have a little fun on that downtime, both with their dancers, as well as with other dance moms so you don't have to be swallowed whole by "waiting."

Advice Christina wishes she'd been given when her daughter started competing? "Save your money – your daughter will want every studio t-shirt, bag, jacket, etc., that's offered. And it's hard to say no!"

She admits the most difficult part about dance can be the chaos of it all – and the stress on your child. "The traveling, rushing around to make costume, hair and makeup changes in ridiculously short amounts of time to make the next performance. Also, some girls are just mean. They can be so cruel to your daughter, and you just want to protect her from all the hatefulness, but you can't, and at the end of the day it's better that she finds her own way to deal with it," says Christina.

Dance Mom Rhonda shares it can be especially tough if you have other active kids in the family. "The hardest part about dance is making the best use of time and money -- especially if there are other children in the family. Dance takes up so much of our time and financial resources that it is sometimes hard to give our two boys an equal portion. We just make sure that we attend all of their events as a family whenever possible, and when it's not possible, we split between events. There have been days when we drove back and forth between ball games or track meets and dance competitions," Rhonda says.

Dance Mom Deanna Thompson would like new dance moms to know they will be sitting a long time. "Bring cushions for the rear end," she advises.

More wise words from Dance Mom Regina, whose daughter has been dancing for five years with Jenks Dance Academy, shares, "Don't stress when they don't get something right the first time. Trust the process."

She also advises moms to make the commitment. "It's not just the money; it's time, but it's totally worth it."

Dr. Marotta reminds us that Company or a School Dance Team is a mini culture so it's our job to help guide that and keep it healthy. "That includes how to know when you need to leave, when it's not going to work and when to say when," she says. "You don't have to drop out in a dramatic way. The parent may need guidance in how to do that well, including why we're leaving."

What about boundary issues? Like many coach/athlete situations, it can often feel like as parents we are completely in the dark, both trying to give our child his/her independence and responsibility, but also keeping a careful watch on when those boundaries are being crossed by any party.

One example Dr. Marotta gave is when a teacher is speaking parallel with kids, often to be friends with them. "That can cause a lot of problems because the authority figure needs to feel and act like an authority," Dr. Marotta warns.

As a whole, when considering a studio or program, Dr. Marotta advises parents to look at the culture of the studio and the specific company, the competitions that they compete in and ask yourselves:

- ➢ is this promoting a healthy body image?
- ➢ is this a positive and encouraging and professional atmosphere?
- ➢ for the dancer: is this where I want to spend my time outside of school and who I want to spend it with?

With a little research, you're sure to find the right fit. Good luck!

chapter 6
How Much is This Going to Cost?

Are kids expensive or what? We faintly remember someone telling us that before we started having them, but goshdarnit, did we listen? Our advice? Brace yourself and budget for it so you won't have too many jaw-dropping surprises.

Hey, that's what we're here for. We're your Reality Check. So, um, moms, are you sitting down? Because dance, like competitive cheer or baseball or football leagues or ice-skating or any number of other activities, is going to cost. It seems even though studios may put out a list in your company packet, we moms may "forget" that when the fees come due, and it feels like something is due every week. Those things sneak up on us.

It can be difficult in rough economic times to devote this much of the family budget to a child's endeavor, so seriously ask yourself if you are (happily) willing to make the investment, because if you're not, and it will make you stressed out and have a panic attack every time a fee is due, you might want to rethink the timing. Planning and open communication is highly recommended.

What you don't want is to mutter profanities under your breath every time a bill comes due. You also don't want your child to feel guilty about the expense, either.

We know you don't want to disappoint your dancer, but if you've filled out our budget sheet below and you simply can't swing it, it's better to not commit than to pull your child out later because payment is an issue.

If you have grandparents who would be willing to help out each month for a portion of it, have that talk with them upfront so that they know what goes into having a Company dancer.

Dance studios are not banks and do not provide loans so you want to stay in good standing with them by paying on time and keeping track of the schedule so the studio doesn't have to track you down. Studios have to pay fees for competitions and conventions and order the costumes so it's important we're keeping the financial commitment we made when we signed the Company contract.

Tip: Ask about fundraising opportunities or create your own!

Our feeling is if you look at it as an investment in their childhood and their happiness, it's easier to swallow than thinking of it as an expense to check off each month.

To that end, here's a handy dandy budget we've put together to help you get the full picture of what your annual expenditures – er, investment – will be. This budget sheet can also be found on our website at www.dancemomsurvivalguide.com.

Annual Dance Budget

CLASSES

Registration Fee	$
Monthly Tuition	$
Dance Clothing	$
Dance Shoes	$
Recital Fee	$
Recital Costume(s)	$
Other	$
Sub-total $	

COMPANY/TEAM DANCE

Tuition	$
Costume(s)	$
T-shirt(s)	$
Team Wear	$
Competition Fee(s)	$
Travel Expenses	$
Lodging	$
Food	$
Other	$
Sub-total $	

CONVENTIONS

Convention Fee(s)	$
Travel Expenses	$
Lodging	$
Food	$
Other	$
Sub-total $	

**TOTAL $**$

When calculating competition fees, remember each dance in a competition has its own fee. For example, there may be a $35 fee per dancer for a group dance. If your dancer participates in four group dances such as hip hop, jazz, lyrical and tap there would be a total of $140 in fees for group dances in one competition. Also, there are additional fees for solos, duets and trios.

A few things to note on the budget. "Other" can swallow you if you let it. As Dance Mom Christina said, it's hard to say no when our dancers want every little thing the studio sells. "Other" for conventions can also mean fun for moms!

We got our hair did (improper language intended) at our last convention and last summer at nationals, we got pedicures. Budgeting in some fun can make your trips more memorable. We favor nice coffee shops, girl talk and maybe even a drink or two at the bar if you have extra time.

Bottom line: know your expenses upfront, stay smart and the expense of dance won't ruin the experience. Who knows? Your dancer could be the next dancing star, YouTube sensation, celebrity choreographer, or studio owner.

They could also simply become a fabulous adult with wonderful memories of dance. That's good, too.

chapter 7
Away we go! Dance camps, conventions and competitions

What makes a dancer better?
What benchmark do dancers use for success?
How can dancers continue to grow in their art?

While dance class may be the lifeblood of the dancer, camps, conventions and competitions are the best way for dancers to spread their wings and fly.

A **Dance Camp** is day or weekend devoted to dance and usually involves guest choreographers. They can be held at host studios or in hotels or convention centers. Dance Camps can be held during "breaks" from school, and often summer camps are the lifeblood of the dance studio for non-Company dancers – and moms who love that their kids can have something fun and productive to do during the summer. They can be a nice gateway to get your dancer to experience a dance style he/she hadn't considered before. It's a low-cost way for a dancer to discover a new dance style without committing to a full year of classes if the dancer isn't "into" that style at the present time.

A **Dance Convention** is a larger venue with more choreographers and can include breakfast/lunch/dinner and end with a showcase. Many conventions award scholarships based on performances, work ethic and attitudes during the convention. Celebrity choreographers are often invited, and it's a hoot for dancers to get to meet and study under choreographers they may have seen on TV or all over the Internet.

A **Dance Competition** is put on by a national dance company who takes their show on the road doing "regional" competitions and ending with a "nationals." When we were newbies, we thought there was only one nationals in dance. Nope. Each company has its own, and studios may choose one close to them or one far away to compete in. The dance competitions may have a celebrity choreographer at the helm. Competitions are a good benchmark for the individual and team dancer because they are scored within their category and then in a larger pool for Overalls.

We found the judging rankings to be confusing since each organization sets it up differently. It's rarely bronze, silver, gold, but rather things like "elite gold", "platinum," "elite platinum." You could get first place and yet get awarded a lower skill ranking. The instructor will typically share the score sheets and judge notes the following week in company class so the dancers will know how they got the score they did (and what to work on before the next competition).

Tips for competition preparedness by Dance instructor Gretchen Ponio

✓ Technique is the key to performance. Without it, dancers look sloppy and unpolished. Again, BALLET!!!

✓ Attitude – Be confident and positive

✓ Preparations – know routines, be solid and comfortable on all timing

✓ Have a costume checklist

Gretchen adds that Conventions are important for dancers to see different choreographers and be exposed to different styles of teaching. "They challenge dancers to learn choreography quickly and learn new techniques for various steps and exercises. And overall, they are a fun experience!" says Gretchen.

Dance Instructor Melissa believes conventions can be a great thing, if taken the right way. "Some studios go to conventions and leave saying, 'I don't like how they teach.' or 'I don't like their style,' or even, 'I didn't feel like I danced enough.' Growing up in California, we were taught that you try the style even if it wasn't our favorite. We were taught to go in there with an open mind because everyone teaches differently. Being able to *adapt* to different styles is what makes a great dancer! Conventions introduce you to the different styles of choreographers! For example, Sonya Tayeh

Contemporary choreography is different than Stacey Tucci Contemporary. You have to learn to adapt! If you can't do a convention open-minded, YOU WILL NOT MAKE IT IN THE PROFESSIONAL WORLD OF DANCE! So many dancers are only one style of dance. Those are the ones who do not succeed in the dance world. Conventions are great, if you go in with an opened mind, and just try."

Dance Instructor Melissa Motte on being prepared

"Being well prepared for competitions? One word: PRACTICE. Some girls believe once a dance is finished, no more practice. *That is when the real work begins.* Cleaning a dance, remembering what you cleaned, and perfecting it. Also, going out there and dancing for YOURSELF. If you go out on stage trying to impress the judges, you get beyond nervous. The judges are wanting to see YOU dance. Yes, they are looking for technique. But a girl with perfect technique vs. a DANCER with perfect technique are totally different. When you step out on stage, your goal is to make the judges see who you are as a dancer. Show them this is your passion, and you will dance your heart out!"

what about dads?

What do dads do at competitions? Truthfully, not that many dads go. If you took a snapshot in a lobby, you'd mostly see a sea of estrogen. Since the teams usually perform the same dances at each competition, a lot of dads go see their dancer once and may skip the rest – at least until recital time. (We know we aren't speaking for everyone!)

A few reasons for this are having other kids at home (and you don't see many siblings due to all the waiting) and having other activities the family attends while the mom and dancer are at the competition. Couple those things with dads (males) not being allowed in the dressing rooms, and it's easy to understand why they feel like a fish out of water much more than even we clueless moms do.

Since nationals can be the most expensive trip and the farthest away, some dads and whole families go thinking they can tack on a family vacation. While we definitely don't want to discourage families from spending time together, we do want to give you the facts that it's tough to balance family time and dance time when dance can take up an extraordinary amount of the week. So unless some family members are driving or flying separately, you may want to consider scheduling a family vacation that doesn't involve the stress and time constraints of competition.

Another idea would be to have the other family members come in the day after the competition is over. Not only will the dancer be relieved that it's over, but he/she can fully concentrate on the family.

Families are encouraged to arrive at least one day prior to competition to ensure you arrive in time and have some downtime, but that also means rehearsal time. Depending on the schedule, you may have an afternoon off, but some dancers, depending on their ages, would much rather spend that time with their dance friends than do something apart from them (and be grumpy the whole time, wishing they were with their friends).

Also it cuts into your precious time off. Having only a few hours in between activities isn't much of a break. And having to "hurry" to get somewhere simply isn't as much fun.

We'd love to hear your thoughts on this on our Facebook page. We recommend going to nationals once with your dance mom BFF or carpooling and seeing how it is once before you decide to pack up all the kids and husband and not have it turn into a *Lampoon's* vacation. We just want your expectations to be in check so you don't leave there thinking, "Worst. Vacation. Ever."

While we're sure there are those dads who rock the hairdos and can fix a costume disaster in no time flat, we often see dads doing one of four things:

• **Sleeping bears.** They typically find the comfiest chair in the lobby and snooze until someone tells them it's time for their dancer to dance.

• **Chauffering.** Not so different than mamas.

• **Carrying the heavy luggage.** Hey, when dad comes, the load lightens a bit, doesn't it?

• **#1 Fans.** Sweet daddy's are the best. They love their daughters and never notice that a foot was turned out or the leap wasn't high enough or they were a second behind everyone else. That's what makes them proud papas.

For a list of fun things to do in those new-to-you cities, we've added the chapter **Dance Moms Just Wanna Have Fun.**

Which nicely leads us to the Dancer Hallie Martin's Packing Checklist for camps, conventions and competitions. One of our favorite benefits of dance is that it can teach our children responsibility and that includes keeping up with their stuff and knowing how to pack.

competition list

Costumes

Hair pieces/accessories (if needed)

Tights

Extra tights

All dance shoes

Jewelry (if needed)

Clothes for after competition

Bobby pins

Hair ties

Nail polish remover

Clear nail polish

Hair spray

Makeup remover

Tissues

Pain meds

Mirror

Water bottle

Healthy snacks

Tampons/pads

Lipstick

Eyeshadow

Eyeliner

Mascara

Foundation

Blush

Lip liner

Safety pins

First Aid Kit

Makeup caddies (such as Caboodles) are the preferred organizational toolbox for competitions. We've seen really elaborate set ups for the changing rooms including racks, chairs, floor-length mirrors and even roll up carpets and privacy screens.

That calls for a pause because the **dressing rooms** can be a bit of an eye-opening surprise for first time dance moms. Studios do not get their own changing rooms and there's usually no time to go to the bathroom to change so this means a "Land Run" of sorts whereby many studios stake out claims in the open rooms and set up camp for the day. A few highlights:

✓   Unless you bring your own chair, you and your dancers will be sitting on the floor.

✓   Lots of girls in various stages of undress. You can bring a curtain for your dancers, but most just change out in the open.

✓   A drink or food caddy is advised, but even if you try to keep things contained, we have seen a lot of spilled drinks on the floor, which means some ruined/stained costumes. Moms should look out for this, because often the dancers are so busy changing, they may not see that they are about to tip over a drink or that one has already spilled on a costume.

✓   Goes without saying, but no males in the dressing room so if mom can't be there, she'll need to ask another dance mom or responsible adult to help keep an eye out or else a female relative.

✓   Depending on your dancer's age and disposition, he/she may not want you in the dressing room with them because either you make them nervous or they feel responsible enough to handle things themselves.

✓   If you're great with hair and makeup, you'll be a huge asset.

✓   The dancers often help each other with hair and makeup, too and may have to do some last minute costume pinning or borrowing. It happens.

chapter 8
communication is key

How to Communicate with the Studio or Dance Team
Tips on Communicating with your Dancer
Keeping You All Organized

Where would we be without smart phones and computers? In this day and age, we're more connected than ever, and it's still possible to miscommunicate and get our lines crossed. As more and more people are shedding landlines and using only mobile phones, it's no wonder that's how moms stay up to date on what's going on in their child's schedules. Every day we get updates from schoolteachers on what's due when. We are definitely communicating at a much different level than our parents did with our teachers and organizations.

Our advice? Stay connected, keep your phone and wi-fi on and keep your calendar handy. Dancers not only can have practice several times a week, but often as competition time draws nearer, more and longer practices are called, and it's imperative to be available when you're at camps and competitions to know when and where your dancer is and what may be needed from you.

On Communicating With The Studio/Team Instructor

✓ Make sure the studio/school has your contact information – email, cell phone, secondary phone number.

✓ Make sure you understand the studio's expectations upfront so you don't get surprised throughout the year.

✓ When the studio hands out paperwork with dates and obligations, go ahead and put those in your calendar and on your dancer's calendar so you can avoid any conflicts, and remember, if you are on the competition team, dancing takes priority over the other activities you may be involved in so likely you'll need to reschedule the conflicting event.

✓ If you aren't sure about something, ask for clarification. We believe most dance studios strive for transparency. Everyone "on the same page" benefits all.

✓ If you aren't getting communication (or it's going only to your dancer), ask that you be added to the call or email list.

✓ Special occasions such as competitions, camps and recitals can be stressful on the studios, so ask how you can help. The older dancers may be asked to step up and mentor or assist the younger dancers, and help from moms is always appreciated.

✓ Dance Moms may be asked to carpool. If you aren't up for that, say so, but often it's standard for moms to take the dancers whose parents are unable to go.

When it comes to **communicating with our dancers**, we like the adage, "everything in its place." Nothing causes Pull-Out-Your-Hairitis like a dancer screaming she can't find her shoes or dance bag or leotard as you're supposed to be out the door to class, or worse, to competition. So a few keys for smoothing out the schedule:

✓ Pick a laundry day where your dancer (or you) will clean all the dance clothes so you'll know when those items are being washed, folded and put away.

✓ Create a special drawer or closet organizer just for dance clothes including those for class and those for weekends and competitions.

✓ Keep dance shoes separate from regular shoes. Unless your child is a Type-A blessing, shoes tend to wander under beds and under piles of other shoes, toys and clothes, so having a place just for dance shoes is wise.

✓ Keep a family calendar where your dancer can see the week's time commitments and if she/he has a smart phone, have them load the schedule on the phone. A family app like Cozi can keep the family informed and ready.

✓ Set a timer so your dancer knows how much time he/she has to be ready for dance. Freak outs can be avoided with enough planning and preparation.

✓ Create a list and get all items for competition weekends (local or for traveling) ready two nights before in case you have to run to the store to get another pair of tights.

✓ Buy two when you can. Of everything. Trust us on this.

✓ Listen twice as much as you talk. Dancers may like to mentally unload after they come home from dance class or rehearsal. They may be frustrated, tired or grumpy. That's perfectly natural. You don't need to do anything other than nod that you hear them and offer to buy them a milkshake. Seriously.

chapter 9
Dance Manners - The Golden Rule and Then Some

List reprinted with permission. Lisa Motsenbocker, studio owner, Dance Phase, Edmond, OK

Dancers show respect for themselves by:
- ✓ Being prompt for class.
- ✓ Being dressed properly for class in the assigned attire, without underwear under leotards, without jewelry other than small earrings, and with shoe strings either tucked in or tied in a knot and cut off.
- ✓ For older dancers hair pulled back in the proper manner.

Dancers show respect for others by:
- ✓ Keeping their hands to themselves during class.
- ✓ Waiting quietly for others to have a turn and for instructions from the teacher.
- ✓ Waiting until the music is finished before entering the classroom if they are late to class.
- ✓ Talking with one another only during Share Time.

Dancers show respect for their teachers and the art form they are learning by:

✓ Being properly dressed and ready for class on time.
✓ Listening when the teacher speaks.
✓ Always standing in the "proper dance stance" while listening to the teacher give combinations or corrections.
✓ Being prepared for their turn.
✓ Always asking before leaving the room for any reason and upon returning enters quietly, never through the dancers who are dancing.

Dancers show respect for the studio by:

✓ Leaving gum, food, or drink outside.
✓ Never hanging or leaning on the barres.
✓ Never running or doing gymnastics in the studio or lobby.
✓ Putting trash in the proper place.
✓ Always keeping all belongings zipped in their dance bag.

Parents show respect for the dance class, teacher, and studio by:

✓ Knocking before entering the classroom if class is in progress.
✓ Making every effort to attend viewing week.
✓ Making sure child has had the opportunity to go to the restroom before entering class.
✓ Having students ready for class before entering the classroom.
✓ Having students at class on time and picking them up promptly after class.

✓ Letting teacher know in advance, if possible, if a student will be absent.

✓ Clearly marking all of their child's items with the child's name and leaving toys at home.

✓ Teaching children to sit quietly while waiting, remembering that the lobby is also a homework area for many dancers.

✓ Teaching children to never run or scream in the studio, waiting areas, or parking lot.

✓ Keeping siblings quietly entertained while waiting in the lobby.

Manners at Competition

➢ Dance Mom Christina adds the importance of not walking in during a performance. You may think you're being quiet and invisible, but you could be blocking a mom or other family member from seeing their dancer dance.

➢ Speak softly in the audience.

➢ Consider covering your glowing screen or turning it off. Yes, you. We see you with your iPad and iPhone out. It's distracting.

➢ Don't keep others waiting, whether that's the studio or other dance moms. Pad extra time in for travel so you're never the one people are waiting for.

➢ Take directions so you don't get lost. We see that happen everywhere we go. Make sure you know which location, because often there are several with similar sounding names.

➢ Don't trust your map. Check with a second source just to be sure your map isn't sending you to the wrong side of town.

chapter 10
Emotional Roller Coaster Ride - Mistakes & More

How to Deal with Emotions in Dance
Stage Fright and Performance Anxiety
Friendships (or not)
Mean Girls, Backstabbing and Bragging Moms

On Making Mistakes by Gretchen Ponio, dance instructor

"I don't know where this phrase came from, but it's a good one. "There are no mistakes, only unexpected solos!"

When dancers forget their choreography whether in a solo or other routine, they need to *always* practice continuing on. To stop and start over in practice isn't helping their memory. Repetition does that.

Making mistakes *will* happen to all dancers. Recognizing what they need to fix and learning how to correct it is the key. This applies when there are errors in technique or timing. Then again, repetition of the proper technique, choreography, and timing will decrease the number of mistakes made.

Onstage Mistakes – "The show must go on!" Improvise until you remember what you were supposed to be doing if you are doing a solo. For a group number, look to someone who is doing your part and catch up! Don't let your face show you've blundered! Judges may never catch it if you pull it off. Wearing it on your face is a dead give away!

On Performance Anxiety with Dr. Marotta

Dr. Marotta, a child and family psychologist, discusses performance anxiety and dealing with stressors:

"Performance anxiety is something they have to work on way before it's time to compete. What are they saying to themselves? How are they critiquing themselves? Help them evaluate their feelings and say, 'How am I going to be different next time?'"

"Some believe in order to be excellent that they have to be anxious, and some really high achieving people use anxiety motivationally; then somewhere it goes wrong." Here's what she suggests we can say to our dancers. "Look at the self-talk. Talk about making the movie in your head. As you're getting ready to perform, say something really kind to yourself and experience liking that feedback and focus on being relaxed. There is an energy that goes into breathing and makes focusing a lot easier. Then let's play it out that you are giving a wonderful performance."

We discussed how dancers naturally critique their

own performances as well as teammates and other dance teams, which she said is understandable and beneficial if done in a constructive and not hurtful way.

She said simply being able to get ready for a performance and then evaluate that performance is a life skill that will come in handy for job interviews or wherever performance is being evaluated, not just with dance.

But back to dance and that automatic "judging" the dancers and moms do.

Dr. Marotta explains, "There's good and bad about it. Tearing another performance down is never okay, but looking for certain things to evaluate is beneficial."

She also wants moms to keep in mind that struggle is not bad and that sometimes parents lose sight of that. "Why can't it be fun and smooth sailing? Life is a struggle and we learn from that. That doesn't mean it's devastating to experience struggle. The other thing to think about is that we're being evaluated *at that point in time*, but this is the one being measured. YOU are not being measured. If self-worth is tied to how you are evaluated, that can lead to performance anxiety."

At this point in the conversation, I shared with Dr. Marotta the oddly wonderful experience at nationals in St. Louis the year before where our dance team had seemed to struggle with energy for the hip hop routine all season long and yet at nationals gave their best performance all year.

Dr. Marotta says that's a great example of why we shouldn't pre-judge things. The dance is a snapshot in time. One performance can be dismal, another mediocre, another extraordinary. What the dancers bring to it each time is what matters.

Dance instructor Melissa says, "The best way to deal with stress as a dancer, is to just breathe. I always tell my dancers when they get frustrated, 'Take a deep breath, and try again. A frustrated mind cannot control a body.' When we psych ourselves out, we have to learn how to breathe and let it go. We make mistakes. If you mess up, learn from it and try again. Getting frustrated doesn't solve anything. Sometimes for me, turning off the lights and just dancing freely calms my nerves.

Dance instructor Gretchen reminds moms that, "There will always be drama of some kind everywhere you go – every sport, every school, every studio. How you handle it is the whole key. Handle things with grace and forgiveness? Or handle things with spite and malice? How people – dancers, parents, teachers, and owners alike – respond to the circumstances around them will determine the reputation of the studio."

Friendships created because of dance can be some of the closest because they spend so much time together. They also share the common bond of their love of dance and won't mind as much when all your dancer wants to do is spend the sleepover practicing routines or stretching "for fun." The downside of dance friendships could be that jealousy can occur if one friend advances beyond the other or gets more recognition. It's important that we discuss these issues with our child if we notice it's happening as that may impact their feelings about themselves or dance. It's natural that some dancers have strengths in one area where others bring it in another. This is another life lesson that our dancers get to experience at an earlier age. It's also important to welcome new dancers into the fold. It can be a scary time for a new dancer to join a group that has already been dancing together. Making them feel welcome can improve chemistry on stage and off. Some teams hold bonding events like pizza and movie nights for the dancers to get together outside of the studio.

Dance Mom friendships can and should be a special time for moms to enjoy time together, without any judgment or bragging or being critical of others. It's natural for moms to want to gossip and critique, but be careful of what is said so it doesn't hurt your reputation, the studio's, or your dancer's.

What about those Mean Dancers (and for that matter Mean Moms)? Best to steer clear and, as my grandma used to say, "Don't get in the mud with the pigs." Sure, the moms do it on reality TV, but this is our own reality, and we don't want our studios or the world of dance to smell like a pigsty, do we?

chapter 11
down the road - college and dancing professionally

So your dancer thinks this might be a life gig? That's cool. What does that look like exactly? College? Dance schools? Moving to New York City or L.A.? Unlike children who might want to be police officers or lawyers or doctors someday, dancing is something they can do professionally while they're young. Though that isn't the focus of this book, we wanted to throw that out there. Some dancers are home-schooled simply so they can have time to go to auditions or be on a TV show and get the extra hours needed to perfect technique, learn new routines and travel for either auditions or with a performance team.

But for the sake of this chapter, we're not going to focus on those "outliers" but on the general dancers who go to school and compete and may want to pursue an advanced education and dance professionally when they are adults.

According to government census data in the field, there are approximately 665 postsecondary institutions that offer dance minor and major programs in the United States.

The National Directory of Dance Schools (compiled by Dance Studios USA) lists over 6,000 private dance studios.

According to the report, dance teachers can hold positions in the following ways:

> ➢ renting studio space as a private contractor

> ➢ gaining employment through a private studio or arts foundation

> ➢ holding a position in public or private elementary or secondary school. (Which would likely require a teaching license.)

Statistical Estimates on Dance Careers in the United States

> ➢ In 2006, self-enrichment educators (including those who teach dance) held 261,000 jobs in America.

> ➢ National averages show they earn between $8.53/hr to over $32.02/hr.

> ➢ Note, some private studios offer their teachers $45.00/hr and higher for advanced curriculum, or company classes, while K-12 dance teachers may be offered salaried positions.

Dancers and Choreographers

According to the findings, most dancers begin their professional career by the age of 18.

In 2006, professional dancers and choreographers made up 40,000 jobs in our country. Of those, 17% were self-employed.

"National averages show that dancers may earn anywhere between $6.62/hr to over $25.75/hr depending on their skill level and type of production. This rate includes rehearsal time, choreography lab time, performance time, and often required time spent in class for company performers. Salary may also depend on location, cost of living, and extent of touring."

➢ Median income of a choreographer in 2009 is approximately $33,000 a year.

➢ Top choreographers directing their own companies may have an annual company operating budget of $5.6 million. However, with operating costs for large companies totaling over $5.2 million, the choreographer may net just over $400,000 each year.

Source: http://www.dancestudiosusa.com

Advice for Going Pro

From Dance Instructor Gretchen Ponio

✓ Get trained or have experience in a variety of dance styles.

✓ Ballet, ballet, ballet! Dancers can't possibly get enough.

✓ Travel to different conventions, schools, experience different teachers.

✓ Difficulty of getting in programs? Depends upon the program.

From Dance Professor Kathleen Redwine

➢ Get the best training possible. Keep working, keep learning. Learn other styles of dance – if you're a ballet dancer, try some tap or jazz or modern dance. Don't be shy about trying a style of dance that's outside your comfort zone like flamenco, hula or belly dance. Stay passionate about your art. Learn other body disciplines like pilates and yoga. Learn to be an artist in dance, not just a technician.

➢ At the college level, dancers need to look at their personal goals in dance and what the school's programs can do to support that. Then other factors can come into play such as scholarships, affordability, etc. By the time a dancer is considering a college degree in dance, he/she should have a pretty good idea of what their individual strengths and weaknesses are, what styles of dance they like, and what they might like to do after they graduate.

➢ A college degree does so many things. In a top-level program, dancers learn from professional level faculty, learn repertoire that will help them get jobs, and often have the opportunity to dance internationally. They also make professional connections. In general, a dance degree helps students get that "polish" and technical improvement necessary to dance professionally. They also usually learn dance pedagogy, or the art of teaching dance, which will both help them get jobs and ensure that the next generation of young dancers has excellent training. A professional dancer's career is short, like a professional athlete's. Having a degree in dance from a major university helps dancers become more well-rounded, educated human beings, and helps them find their second career. Many of our dance majors have a strong minor in another field, or even double major. We've had dance majors study finance, marketing, public relations, art, pre-med and many other areas.

A few more questions for Professor Redwine:

Do all schools of dance at the collegiate level require auditions?

KR: All the programs that I'm aware of require an audition.

What are dance instructors looking for in dancers 18+?

KR: Each college dance program has their own focus, but in general, we're all looking for wonderful dancers who can also be successful in a university environment.

What tips do you have on dancers taking care of themselves?

KR: Mind/body/wellness

From Instructor/Dance Major Melissa Motte

The third-year dance major says sticking with it is key.

➤ "Getting into a college dance program isn't too hard depending on your training background, but staying in it is. College dance programs accept you based off of if they are able to TRAIN YOU. If your technique is way off, you might not get in. But if they see you have some technique and you're trainable, they will accept you. You don't have to be perfect. But if you DO get accepted, staying in is the hard part. It is HARD WORK and takes a lot of TIME and DEDICATION!!

➤ Class attendance and improvement are the two biggest things. If they see you are not improving, they will tell you, "Hey, we need to start seeing improvements soon." If they don't, they may suggest a different major maybe, or remove you from the program. Being a dance major is a blast, but hard. Your body needs rest, and you have to be able to balance normal school work, too.

➤ To prepare for college dance — technique, technique, technique. Also be in shape, and start eating healthy. Listen to your studio teachers, especially if they are a dance major currently or have been one.

> Scholarships are everywhere!! You just have to search for them. There are even websites just for dancers!

From Dance Mom Lauren

> Career planning is also tricky. I can't tell you how many times I've wished for a crystal ball to give me a glimpse of the future! My son is at an age right now (14) when he's beginning to get noticed. For example, when he was at one big-name SI (Summer Intensive) audition recently, he was offered a scholarship on the spot, and they were really trying to talk him in to attending their program. Then, a few days later a famous boarding school/conservatory offered him a full-ride scholarship (tuition, room, board) and expressed a lot of interest in him. I thought he had decided to go there, but then yesterday at a competition, the director of different ballet company pulled us aside to offer my son a full scholarship for the summer, telling us that he is just what they are looking for for their company in the future.

> Do the decisions we make now affect his career in the future? I have no idea! But it does sometimes keep me up at night wondering and worrying.

Scholarship Information Online

Keep in mind that scholarship information will be readily accessible on college and summer intensive websites, so check there first. If you already know which colleges or programs you are interested in, visit them early and try to meet the faculty and get a tour. It might be just the thing your dancer needs to stay motivated while in middle school and high school. It's also a good idea to talk to people who have attended the program recently to get an unbiased opinion of the school.

Chapter 12
Dance Moms Just Wanna Have Fun

What? You didn't think we could end the book with shipping your darling dancer off to college or Broadway, did you? No way. We have a bit more fun in store.

Here's the thing: we think a lot of moms look downright miserable at dance conventions, camps and nationals. We know that glassy-eyed look when we see it, and no, it's not from martinis at happy hour. To keep things lively and to make wonderful memories with your dancer and dance group, we've come up with a list of places to visit in ten cities and our very own "dance mom bucket list." You know, stuff to do before you kick the dance bucket for good. Enjoy!

St. Louis

1. **Gateway Arch** – gatewayarch.com – The Core of Discovery, St. Louis, MO 63102
2. **Jilly's Cupcake Bar & Café** – jillyscupcakebar.com – 8509 Delmar Boulevard, St. Louis, MO 63124
3. **City Museum** – citymuseum.org – 701 North 15th Street, St. Louis, MO 63103
4. **The Magic House,** St. Louis Children's Museum – magichouse.org - 516 S. Kirkwood Road, St. Louis, MO 63122
5. **Grant's Farm** – grantsfarm.com - 10501 Gravois Rd, Saint Louis, MO 63123
6. **Saint Louis Zoo** *free admission* - stlzoo.org - One Government Drive, St. Louis, MO 63110
7. **Delmar Loop** *entertainment and shopping district* - VisitTheLoop.com – 6504 Delmar Boulevard, St. Louis, MO 63130
8. **Ted Drewes Frozen Custard** – teddrewes.com – 2 locations – 6726 Chippewa, St. Louis, MO 63109 (February-December) 4224 South Grand Boulevard, St. Louis, MO 63111 (Summer only)
9. **Six Flags St. Louis** – sixflags.com – 4900 Six Flags Road, Eureka, MO 63025
10. **Blue's City Deli** – bluescitydeli.com - 2438 McNair Avenue, Saint Louis, MO 63104

Atlanta

1. **Swan Coach House Restaurant** - swancoachhouse.com - 3130 Slaton Drive Northwest, Atlanta, GA 30305
2. **Fox Theatre** – foxtheatre.org – 660 Peachtree Street NE, Atlanta, GA 30308
3. **Center for Puppetry Arts** – puppet.org - 1404 Spring Street, NW at 18th, Atlanta, GA 30309
4. **Georgia Aquarium** – georgiaaquarium.org - 225 Baker Street NW, Atlanta, GA 30313
5. **World of Coca-Cola** – worldofcoca-cola.com - 121 Baker St NW, Atlanta, GA 30313
6. **High Museum of Art** – high.org - 1280 Peachtree Street, N.E, Atlanta, GA 30309
7. **CamiCakes Cupcakes** – camicakes.com - 2221 Peachtree Rd, Suite B, Atlanta, GA 30309
8. **Atlantic Station** – atlanticstation.com - 1380 Atlantic Drive, Suite 14250, Atlanta, GA 30363
9. **Pasta Da Pulcinella** – pastadapulcinella.com - 1123 Peachtree Walk, Atlanta, GA 30309
10. **Murphy's** – murphys-atlanta-restaurant.com - 997 Virginia Avenue , Atlanta, GA 30306

Anaheim, CA

1. **Segerstrom Center for the Arts** – scfta.org - 600 Town Center Drive, Costa Mesa, CA 92626
2. **Huntington Beach** – surfcityusa.com
3. **Anaheim GardenWalk** – anaheimgardenwalk.com – 321 W. Katella Avenue, Anaheim, CA 92802
4. **Slaters 50/50** *burgers* - slaters5050.com – 6362 E. Santa Ana Canyon Road, Anaheim Hills, CA 92807
5. **Disneyland** – Disneyland.disney.go.com – 1313 S. Disneyland Drive, Anaheim, CA 92802
6. **Knott's Berry Farm** – knotts.com - 8039 Beach Boulevard, Buena Park, CA USA 90620
7. **Mama Cozza's** – mamacozzas.com - 2170 West Ball Road, Anaheim, CA 92804
8. **Baci di Firenze Trattoria** – bacianaheim.com - 416 N Lakeview Ave, Anaheim, CA 92807
9. **Flightdeck Air Combat Center** – flightdeck1.com - 1650 S. Sinclair St., Anaheim, CA 92806
10. **In-N-Out** – in-n-out.com - 600 South Brookhurst, Anaheim, CA 92804

Oklahoma City

1. **Oklahoma City Thunder NBA game** – thunder.nba.com – Chesapeake Energy Arena, 100 W Reno Ave, Oklahoma City, OK 73102
2. **Science Museum Oklahoma** – sciencemuseumok.org – 2100 NE 52nd Street, Oklahoma City, OK 73111
3. **Oklahoma City Museum of Art** – okcmoa.com - 415 Couch Drive, Oklahoma City, OK 73102
4. **Bricktown Canal** – bricktownokc.com –
5. **Vast** *fine dining atop Devon Tower* - vastokc.com – 333 W. Sheridan Avenue, Oklahoma City, OK 73102
6. **Pinkitzel Cupcakes and Candy** – pinkitzel.com - 150 N. EK Gaylord Boulevard, Oklahoma City, OK 73102
7. **Cattlemen's Steakhouse in Historic Stockyard City** – cattlemensrestaurant.com - 1309 S Agnew Ave Oklahoma City, OK 73108
8. **Pops** – route66.com - 660 W. Highway 66, Arcadia, OK 73007
9. **Nikkellette's Café** * known for their Raspberries 'N Crème cake* - raspberriesncreme.com – 2925 Lakeside Circle, Oklahoma City, OK 73120
10. **Inspirations** *tea room & dining* - inspirationstearoom.com -   2118 West Edmond Road, Edmond, OK 73003

seattle

1. **Pike Place Market** – pikeplacemarket.org – located at 1st and Pike in Downtown Seattle
2. **Pacific Northwest Ballet** – pnb.org - 301 Mercer Street, Seattle, WA 98109
3. **Chihuly Garden & Glass** – chihulygardenandglass.com – 305 Harrison Street, Seattle, WA 98109
4. **Cupcake Royale** – cupcakeroyale.com – 1111 East Pike Street, Seattle, WA 98122 (also other locations in Seattle)
5. **Molly Moon's** *ice cream* - mollymoonicecream.com – 1622 ½ N. 45th Street, Seattle, WA 98107 (also other locations in Seattle)
6. **Space Needle** – spaceneedle.com – 400 Broad Street, Seattle, WA 98109
7. **Tutta Bella Neapolitan Pizzeria** – tuttabella.com – 4918 Rainier Avenue South, Seattle, WA 98118
8. **Bakery Nouveau** – bakerynouveau.com - 4737 California Ave SW Seattle, WA 98116
9. **Ride the ferry to Bainbridge Island** – wsdot.com
10. **Museum of Flight** – museumofflight.org - 9404 East Marginal Way S. Seattle, WA 98108

Nashville, TN

1. **Country Music Hall of Fame and Museum** – countrymusichalloffame.org - 222 5th Avenue South, Nashville, TN 37203
2. **The Pancake Pantry** – thepancakepantry.com - 1796 21st Avenue South, Nashville, TN 37212
3. **Grand Ole Opry** – opry.com - 2804 Opryland Drive, Nashville, TN 37214
4. **Frothy Monkey Coffeehouse** – frothymonkeynashville.com - 2509 12th Avenue South, Nashville, TN 37204
5. **Loveless Café** – lovelesscafe.com - 8400 Highway 100, Nashville, TN 37221
6. **Bluebird Café** – bluebirdcafe.com - 4104 Hillsboro Pike, Nashville, TN 37215
7. **The Hermitage, Home of President Andrew Jackson** – thehermitage.com - 4580 Rachel's Lane, Nashville, TN 37076
8. **The Frist Center for Visual Arts** – fristcenter.org - 919 Broadway Nashville, TN 37203
9. **The Cupcake Collection** – thecupcakecollection.com - 1213 6th Avenue North, Nashville, TN 37208
10. **Old Made Good** *vintage and locally made goods* – oldmadegood.com - 3701B Gallatin Pike, Nashville, TN 37216

Jacksonville, FL

1. The **Beach!**
2. **Friendship Fountain** - 1015 Museum Circle, Jacksonville, FL 32207
3. **Alhambra Theatre & Dining** – alhambrajax.com - 12000 Beach Boulevard, Jacksonville, FL 32246
4. **The French Pantry** - 6301 Powers Ave, Jacksonville, FL 32217
5. **Jacksonville Zoo & Gardens** – jacksonvillezoo.org - 370 Zoo Pkwy, Jacksonville, FL 32218
6. **Sweet By Holly** – sweetbyholly.com - 4624 Town Crossing Drive, Suite 137, Jacksonville, FL 32246
7. **The Dreamette** *ice cream* - 3646 Post Street, Jacksonville, FL 32205
8. **The Cummer Museum of Art & Gardens** – cummer.org - 829 Riverside Avenue, Jacksonville, FL 32204
9. **Museum of Science and History** – themosh.org - 1025 Museum Circle, Jacksonville, FL 32207
10. Day trip to **Amelia Island** – ameliaisland.com

Dallas

1. **Dallas World Aquarium** – dwazoo.com - 1801 North Griffin Street, Dallas, TX 75202
2. **Dallas Museum of Art** – dm-art.org - 1717 North Harwood, Dallas, TX 75201
3. **Dallas Arboretum & Botanical Gardens** – dallasarboretum.org - 8525 Garland Road, Dallas, TX 75218
4. **The Sixth Floor Museum** – jfk.org - 411 Elm Street, Dallas, TX 75202
5. **McKinney Avenue Trolley** – mata.org
6. **Society Bakery** – societybakery.com - 3426 B Greenville Avenue, Dallas, TX 75206
7. **Galleria** *upscale shopping mall* - galleriadallas.com - 13350 Dallas Pkwy, Dallas, TX 75240
8. **Avila's Restaurant** *Mexican* - avilasrestaurant.com - 4714 Maple Avenue, Dallas, TX 75219
9. **All Good Café** – allgoodcafe.com - 2934 Main Street, Dallas, TX 75226
10. **Medieval Times Dinner & Tournament** – medievaltimes.com - 2021 North Stemmons, Dallas, TX 75207

Denver

1. Afternoon tea at **The Brown Palace Hotel and Spa** – brownpalace.com – 321 17th Street, Denver, CO 80202
2. **Snooze** *breakfast/brunch* - snoozeeatery.com – 2262 Larimer Street, Denver, CO 80205
3. **Water World** – waterworldcolorado.com - 8801 N. Pecos Street, Federal Heights, CO 80260
4. **Tattered Cover Book Store** – tatteredcover.com – 1628 16th Street, Denver, CO 80202
5. **The Denver Center for the Performing Arts** – denvercenter.org - Speer & Arapahoe, Denver, CO 80204
6. Hiking at **Mount Evans** – mountevans.com -
7. **Kirkland Museum of Fine & Decorative Art** – kirklandmuseum.org – 1311 Pearl Street, Denver, CO 80203
8. **Cake Crumbs** – cake-crumbs.com - 2216 Kearney Street, Denver, CO 80207
9. **Children's Museum of Denver** – mychildsmuseum.org - 2121 Children's Museum Drive, Denver, CO 80211
10. **Molly Brown House Museum** – mollybrown.org – 1340 Pennsylvania Street, Denver, CO 80203

New York City

1. **Metropolitan Museum of Art** – metmuseum.org - 1000 Fifth Avenue, New York, NY 10028
2. **Statue of Liberty** – nps.gov - Liberty Island, New York City, NY 10004
3. **Empire State Building** – esbnyc.com - 350 Fifth Avenue, Between 33rd and 34th Streets, New York City, NY 10118
4. **Magnolia Bakery** – magnoliabakery.com - 401 Bleecker Street, New York, NY 10014
5. **FAO Schwarz** *toy store* - fao.com - *767 5th Avenue @ 58th Street, New York, NY 10153*
6. **Dylan's Candy Bar** – dylanscandybar.com - 1011 3rd Avenue, New York, NY 10065
7. **Central Park** – centralparknyc.org -
8. **Times Square** – timessquarenyc.org -
9. **Good Enough to Eat** – goodenoughtoeat.com - 483 Amsterdam Avenue, New York, NY 10024
10. **American Girl Store** – Americangirl.com – 609 Fifth Avenue, New York, NY 10017

Additional Source:
http://www.bls.gov/ooh/Entertainment-and-Sports/Dancers-and-choreographers.htm

About the Authors

Jill Martin (left) has a B.A. in Child Development from Harding University. While at Harding, she fell in love with a handsome young man as they served together on a mission trip to Houston's inner city. Soon after, they married and now have four fabulous children, one of whom is a dancer.

Malena Lott is a married mother of three in in the Midwest, where she is a dance mom, den mom, brand strategist and author. She is the author of four women's fiction novels including *Fixer Upper* and *Something New*. See all of her titles on her website: www.malenalott.com Connect with her @malenalott on Twitter and Instagram and on Facebook at www.facebook.com/malenalottbooks.

Jill and Malena invite you to connect with them on their Facebook page and Twitter @dancesurvival.

http://www.facebook.com/dancemomsurvivalguide.

More Buzz Books you may enjoy:

TMI Mom: Oversharing My Life by Heather Davis
(humor, family)
Next Left by Dani Stone, an ebook novelette, fiction
Something New by Malena Lott, fiction
PR Rock Star by Cyndy Hoenig (business)
The Little Brand That Could by Malena Lott (business)
Distortion by Lucie Smoker (fiction: crime, mystery)

For the full list of titles and to get to know our authors,
visit www.BuzzBooksUSA.com.

Dance Forever Gear
visit dancemomsurvivalguide.com and facebook.com/dancemomsurvivalguide to buy shirts, tote bags and sweatpants

Made in the USA
San Bernardino, CA
08 January 2014